Sharron Davies

Julia Holt

Published in association with The Basic Skills Agency

Hodder & Stoughton
A MEMBER OF THE HODDER HEADLINE GROUP

Acknowledgements

Cover: Colin Mason.

Photos: p. 5 © Hulton Getty; pp. 8, 10, 14 Solo Syndication Ltd;
pp. 17, 20, 25, 27 Press Association News Photo Library.

Orders: please contact Bookpoint Ltd, 39 Milton Park, Abingdon, Oxon OX14 4TD. Telephone: (44) 01235 400414, Fax: (44) 01235 400454. Lines are open from 9.00–6.00, Monday to Saturday, with a 24 hour message answering service. Email address: orders@bookpoint.co.uk

British Library Cataloguing in Publication Data
A catalogue record for this title is available from The British Library

ISBN 0 340 74735 8

First published 1999
Impression number   10 9 8 7 6 5 4 3 2 1
Year   2004 2003 2002 2001 2000 1999

Copyright © 1999 Julia Holt

Cover photo from London Features.
Typeset by Fakenham Photosetting Ltd, Fakenham, Norfolk.
Printed in Great Britain for Hodder & Stoughton Educational, a division of Hodder Headline Plc, 338 Euston Road, London NW1 3BH by Redwood Books, Trowbridge, Wiltshire.

Contents

Sharron Davies
is the golden girl of British swimming.

In her long career
of over 20 years,
she has broken and rebroken
over 200 British records

She was twice voted
sportswoman of the year.

She is Britain's most successful
all-round female swimmer.
These days she also has
a successful second career.

1 Early Days

Sharron Elizabeth
was born on 1 November 1962
in Plymouth, Devon.

As a little girl she was keen
on ballet and horse riding.
But at six years old
she learned to swim.

Little did her parents know
that Sharron was at the start
of a long career.

By the time Sharron
was ten years old
she was training every day.

Her parents
and her young twin brothers
were a big support to her.

All sports done at the top level
cost a lot of money.
Sponsors were hard to find.

Sharron had to find the money
for kit, travel and coaching.

Sharron first swam for Britain
at the age of 11.
She was the only one in her team
to win.

That year her father, Tony,
became her coach.
She had her sights set
on the next Olympics,
in Canada, in 1976.

At 13 years old
she was the youngest member
of the 1976 Olympic team.
But she didn't look young
because she was 5 foot 7 inches tall.

Sharron swam for Britain in the 1976 Olympics.
She was only 13 years old.

Sharron enjoyed the Montreal Olympics
apart from being sent to bed at 10pm.
It was good training
for the 1980 Olympics.

When she was 15 years old
Sharron was sent to boarding school.
This gave her the chance to swim
and to study.

She was good at Maths
but swimming
was more important.

2 Medals

In 1978 Sharron was back in Canada
for the Commonwealth Games.

She won two gold medals
for the 200 metre and 400 metre
individual medleys.

Sharron was voted
sportswoman of the year
by the sporting press.
She is very proud of the award
because it's not just for swimmers.

Sharron in 1978 with some of her trophies.

In the 1980 Moscow Olympics
Sharron won a silver medal
in the 400 metre individual medley.

Again she was voted
sportswoman of the year.

Sharron then chose to have
a nine-year break
from swimming in big competitions.

Sharron with some of her medals.

But she came back in 1989
to break more records
and win more medals.

In the 1990 Commonwealth Games
she won a silver and a bronze,
and she was the ladies' captain.

Two years later
she broke her own 12 year record
for the 400 metre individual medley.

Sharron was the oldest member
of the Barcelona Olympic team
in 1992.
She didn't come back with a medal.
Instead she came back
with a new boyfriend.
The top runner, Derek Redmond.

Sharron didn't swim well
and Derek tore a hamstring.
So they spent the time
being unhappy together.

When they got home
Derek proposed to Sharron
outside a fish and chip shop.

3 Marriage

1993 was a fantastic year
for Sharron.

She married Derek
on St Valentine's Day.
Sharron chose that day
so that Derek will always remember it.

She wore a short,
cream and black dress
with long tails
and a tall hat with a veil.

Later, when they both had time,
they had a lovely honeymoon
in the Caribbean.

Sharron and Derek on their wedding day.

Also in 1993
Sharron was awarded
the MBE by the Queen.
She was given the award
for all she had done
for Britain and for sport.

Sharron wore a green wool suit
and she took her Mum and Dad
when she met the Queen.
They were very proud of her.

After the awards
Sharron took her Mum and Dad
for a slap-up meal
to thank them for all they had done.

Last but not least
Sharron had her first child
in November 1993.
They called him Elliott.

The family live
in a beautiful converted barn
in the Cotswolds.
They have two cats,
a dog called Bella
and a horse called Sly.

Sharron and Derek with their son Elliott.

4 A New Career

Sharron retired from swimming
and took up a career in media.

She has been in over
80 different TV shows
as a guest or a presenter.
She is a regular commentator
for sports programmes.
She has also written books
and made a fitness video.

Swimming is more or less
an injury free sport.
Sharron didn't suffer
any major injuries in her career.

Then in 1995
she joined the TV show
Gladiators.
She was called Amazon.
Sharron enjoyed working on the show
until she snapped a knee ligament.
She had to leave the show.

Since then Sharron has had
five operations on that ligament
and it still isn't right.

As Gladiator Amazon in 1995.

In between her media jobs
Sharron enjoys riding her horse
in three-day events
and watching Derek play rugby.

Sharron started a new career,
designing the insides of houses.
She set up her own company
called 'Making Waves'.
Design has always been
one of her interests.

Life sounds fantastic
for Sharron and her family.
But in 1997
she was the target of a parcel bomb.
Happily, no-one was hurt.

It was sent to her by racists
because she is married
to a black man.
Three racists were sent to prison
for sending the parcel bomb.
This has not split up
Sharron and Derek,
it has made them stronger.

Sharron's second baby
was born in June 1998.
They called her Grace Elizabeth.

Sharron chose to have
a water birth at home
so that Derek and Elliott
could help.

Grace was born in a pool
set up in the kitchen.
Sharron and Elliott
sat in the pool
and Derek kept the water warm
and made cups of tea.

Sharron loves being a Mum
but she doesn't like being pregnant.
She is used to being super fit
and in control of her body.
She was very glad
to see her feet again after Grace was born.

Sharron was soon back to work.
In September 1998
she commented
on the Commonwealth Games for TV.

Sharron took four month old Grace to work
in October 1998.

5 Honoured

When Sharron was awarded her MBE
the Queen thanked her
for all her hard work
and wished her luck
with all her other interests.

It seems that
she doesn't need much luck
because she puts as much energy
into her media work
as she did into her swimming.

Sharron shows off her MBE
outside Buckingham Palace.

In people's minds
Sharron still represents
the best of swimming.

She still holds the British record
for the 400 metre individual medley.
She is still Britain's most successful
all-round female swimmer.